INTRODUCTION

Set between Bristol and Bath, but physically closer to the latter is the small town of Saltford, and the two small villages of Corston and Newton St Loe, and it is these three communities which are the subject of this book. Historically all are very old, having each appeared as settlements of one description or another in the Domesday Book, with Saltford being described as land for ten ploughs, with around twenty-five or so families, one of whom was almost certainly a miller, as a mill is recorded in that document. Until around three hundred years ago, the River Avon was tidal throughout the parish and, accordingly, in the area now known as The Shallows, it was possible to be able to ford the river and cross over into Gloucestershire. Thus with the added bonus of there being fertile soil in the area, it easily became an ideal spot to create, either by design or by accident, the beginning of a settlement on the south side of the river, and was the reason for its name although, as far as is known there is no connection with salt. At the time of the Domesday Book, it was spelt Sanford, whilst in the sixteenth century it had become Sartfford, and thus today's name has probably arisen as a result of bad spelling and poor pronunciation. It has been said on more than one occasion that Saltford has little or no history, but that would be to deny the fact that it has remained a place of increasing habitation for well over a millennium. It is true that historically Saltford has been something of a backwater with no earth shattering events of national importance having occurred within its boundary but with a little delving snippets of interest can always be found. We already know that Saltford was mentioned in the Domesday Book and, additionally, that the Manor of Saltford was at one time annexed to the honour of Gloucester, and was held as such by the family of Bayouse during the reign of Henry lll, and Edward l, before moving to the Rodney's who continued to hold the manor throughout the reign of Queen Elizabeth l after which time the manor became the property of the Duke of Chandos. Of the Manor House itself, it is believed to be one; if not the, oldest inhabited house in Somerset, and one of the eldest in the country, with many Norman features. The church of St Mary the Virgin, which is to the east of the manor house, was probably constructed during the twelfth century, and almost certainly occupies the site of an earlier Saxon church. For many people, today's Saltford represents a somewhat sprawling dormitory community with a very busy main road running through the centre and virtually cutting the town in two. Two hundred years or more ago, Saltford would have looked to the casual observer much different, with the main road and the village huddled along the hill as it fell towards the river and along the river itself. Closer examination will today show the original quaintness of the village as it tumbled down the hill along High Street, skirting both the manor house and the church, with clusters of homes and other buildings spreading out around the hillside but still keeping close to that main thoroughfare, before swinging right past the fording point, and then on through what was very often little more than muddy tracks towards Bath. It was probably during the seventeenth century when Saltford "hit the headlines" as the great rebellion of 1685 brushed by for one brief moment in time. With the Duke of Monmouth keen to pocket Bristol as his greatest prize, and with his advisors telling him to attack the city from the east, he brought his supporters around from Shepton Mallet in a wide loop, which took him south of Bath, and then through Saltford to camp just outside of Keynsham. How many of his troops were camped at Saltford has not been recorded, nor is it absolutely certain that the Duke gave Saltford anything more than a cursory glance, as for reasons best known to himself, he certainly did not try to ford the river at Saltford, preferring instead to use the County Bridge two miles or so down river. Some twenty-seven years later, in the September of 1702, Queen Ann made her gout ridden way through Saltford from Bath as she tried to fulfil the (cont'd on inside back cover)

KEYNSHAM FROM THE WELLS ROAD   K-8519

The picture on the left is the view looking down most of the length of Steel Mills from the Wellsway, across the Chew Bridge to the cluster of houses at the bottom of Dapps Hill. On the left-hand side of the skyline are the buildings which originally formed the Keynsham Workhouse and then subsequently the Keynsham Hospital. c1958

For hundreds of years Keynsham benefited from the use of water-power and had many mills all of which would have, at various times, been agriculturally based for the production of flour, cloth and malt, but subsequently they were used in connection with the production of brass. This particular mill had a renewal of life at the turn of the last century when it became involved with the production of dyewoods and chemicals. c1935.

LOGWOOD MILLS KEYNSHAM.   A7735.

Most of the inhabitants of Dapps Hill have been gathered together by the photographer to take this charming animated picture of life as it used to be in this little backwater of Keynsham around Chew Bridge. Somehow he has managed to encourage many of them to come out into the sunshine as a tiny bit of history is frozen in time before their World was to change forever. c1910.

Temple Street, Keynsham.

With an absence of any road vehicle our view of Temple Street is unhindered as we look back in time to when life was so very different. Bath Hill drops down to the left; with the six-sided weighbridge perched on top of the hill where it might cause the most hindrance. Behind is the right-hand end of Cheapside sadly wiped away by the local planners act of vandalism in the 1960's. On the extreme right is the porticoes entrance to the *LAMB & LARK HOTEL*. With many children posed along the street the photographer somehow managed to get the majority of them looking at the camera all at the same time. C1904

Two views of Bath Road Keynsham on its way towards Saltford; with on the right a picture taken when the road was relatively quiet and infrequently used by motor vehicles. This aspect shows the magnificent trees along the side of the road between the turnings of Unity Road, and Broadmead Lane. c1935.

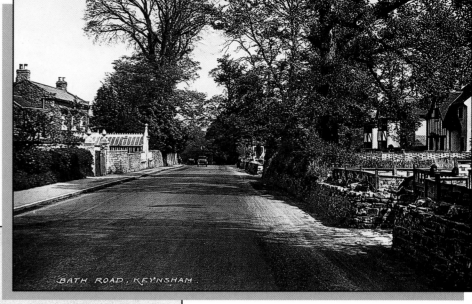

BATH ROAD, KEYNSHAM.

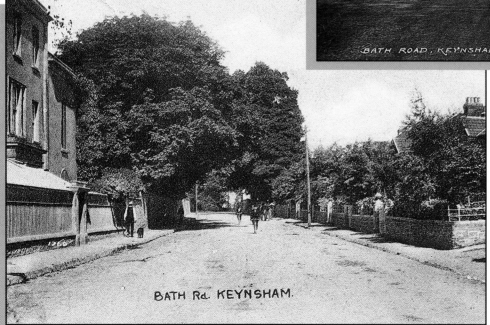

BATH Rd. KEYNSHAM.

On the left is an earlier picture of the main road at its junction with Chandag Road, taken in an era when it was perfectly safe to cycle in the middle of the highway. The trees are at their summer best on a hot sunny day around. c1911.

5

39079. NORMAN ROAD, SALTFORD.

This c1935 view on the left has been taken about half-way along Norman Road, when that road still had a great deal of countryside around it. With just one parked vehicle (CHY 762) in an otherwise deserted road, the shadowy shape can be seen of the Saltford Evangelical Church, [having now been demolished, despite the fact that one of the original conditions was that the hall and land had been left to the village for as long as the building was being continually used as a place of worship]

Although this right-hand view will be easily recognized as Norman Road, it was originally known from the mid nineteenth century as Boyd Lane. Its name was changed to Mission Hall Lane in the 1890's, and remained as such until 1928 when the present name was introduced. The reason for the intermediate change is due to the large building on the left, which had been constructed around 1872 as a workingmen's hall for Gospel Meetings. Some twenty-year's later, the title was shortened to The Mission Hall, and the change in the name of the road followed soon after. In this c1920 picture, workmen appear to be laying paving stones on the right-hand side.

Mission Hall Lane, Saltford

Tunnel House, Saltford.

This substantial building is known as Tunnel House due to the fact that it sits diagonally over Brunel's Saltford tunnel, which conveys the main Bristol [TM] to Paddington railway line. Note the false window built in this way to harmonize with the style of the building, but blocked up to save "Window Tax". C1904. Below we can see the same building peering through the trees as it stands at the junction of Norman Road, Beech Road and High Street. At this point it is possible to see the grass triangle on which the War Memorial is to be erected twenty-two years or so later. c1908.

The newly erected WW1 war Memorial wreathed with flowers and a laurel wreath, stands in the middle of the grass triangle as seen on the adjoining picture. c1923.

WAR MEMORIAL. SALTFORD

7

A pristine War Memorial in the shape of a Celtic cross stands proudly in the centre of its fenced triangular patch of green which the local authority has craftily arranged so that it can double up as a traffic island, without the need to set up "keep-left" signs. With the picture taken from Beech Road, Tunnel House is to the left of the large central tree whilst, on the right, behind yet another tree, stands the proud Saltford Manor. Although the card from which the picture is taken was posted in 1951, the photograph was almost certainly taken c1930.

Although not the best of pictures this shot of the War Memorial taken from Norman Road whilst looking down High Street is worthy of inclusion because of its rarity. The painted metal fencing can clearly be seen at a time when it was quite safe to stroll along the middle of the highway provided, of course, you did not follow exactly in the footsteps of the horse that had preceded you. c1927.

THE VILLAGE, SALTFORD.

We have now gone back in time as well as having moved the position of the camera, to capture this fascinating view of the top end of the High Street. With the gate entrance to Saltford Manor on the left, the photographer has managed to gather together many of the local school children and placed them in a statuesque position all facing the camera and perhaps too frightened to move. On the right-hand side, the trees still grow in a field, yet to have a rank of houses constructed along its edge, which means that there is at present no need for a pavement. c1904.

39080. HIGH STREET, SALTFORD.

Some thirty years or more have past since the previous picture was taken, and the camera has changed the angle to show a much more modern High Street. The gate to the manor house can be seen, but building changes have been made to the opposite piece of ground, with the construction of a rank of terraced houses. There are just two cars [one registered DAE29] and a bicycle in this peaceful scene, which is unlikely to be replicated today, all of which are parked outside Batstone & Williams, whose shop board hanging on the front of the building claims them to be "High class provisioners" ~~ phone Saltford 763. Note the leaning School sign on the right, warning the occasional and possibly unwary motorists of what lay ahead. c1935.

NORMAN HOUSE, SALTFORD.

Originally built as a row of cottages during the seventeenth century, Norman House is the result of merging the individual dwellings into one habitation. The above picture, which appears to have been taken on a fine hot sunny day, shows a workman with pickaxe looking more than happy to be having a break whilst his picture is being taken, little did he know that this moment in time would be frozen for ever. c1904

One of the original and important shops in the High Street, "Coombes" a general store selling a variety of products although, by the look of the window display, the stocking level of the shop was quite small. The lady in the picture is possibly Mrs. Coombe, but who are the two gentlemen and child? No longer a shop, the bay window has gone, and the front has been rendered, with the property known as Collins Buildings. c1904.

SALTFORD SCHOOL.

The village school with the children, their teachers and the local vicar have been grouped together in their Sunday best. Whilst the photographer captures the architectural style of Queen's School, constructed around 1870, at the high cost of £1,200, with the Rev. C.R.Ward having generously donated much of this money. The school itself was built on land where previously an old gabled thatched roofed cottage had stood. To the right of the school is part of Queen's Square, with part of Manor House Farm in the background. c1904.

St. Mary the Virgin is the parish church of Saltford having been originally built during the thirteenth century, the whole fabric of the building underwent major restoration in 1832, as seen here from the churchyard c1924.

The interior of the church taken around the same time, showing its single aisle, boxed pews, and on the left can be seen the white marble monument in memory of the late Rev. Haviland John Hiley and Eleanor his wife.

Street and Post Office, Saltford.

On the extreme right of the left-hand picture is the end property of a rank of cottages built around 1745 and known as Churchview Cottages. The large building to their right is Brass Knocker House, which was formally an inn when a certain Ann Smith lived there. At a later date during the 1890's it became the village butchers shop. Once again the photographer has managed to gather together the local children to pose for him c1904

This is a similar view taken from the other side of the road some seventeen years and a World War later. Brass Knocker House is now masquerading as the village Post Office, on one of those quiet days in Saltford's past. Built around 1826, on land known as Green Batch, the house was originally called Mount Cottage. c1920.

In this interesting picture of the *Bird in Hand,* the photographer has persuaded the landlord, Edwin Packer, and a number of his regulars, plus one or two visitors, to interrupt their drinking time and step outside to have their picture taken in the bright late afternoon sunshine. [Take particular note of the middle group of four as they are also in the next picture.] In pride of place is what is believed to be a 1920 BSA V twin 1,000cc motorcycle {Reg. No AD6503] and to its right is a 1921 Flat Twin 4HP Douglas 598cc bike. Originally built as two cottages, the property was converted into a single public house at the time that the Midland Railway was being constructed, as there were at the time a large number of navies with a preponderance of dry throats that needed constant lubrication. c1925.

A short while before the previous picture had been taken, the same photographer arranged this shot, to include the four cyclists who were to re-appear in his picture of the outside of the *Bird in Hand,* the latter having no doubt already quenched their thirst before they were to pose for the second time. Here we see the lower end of the High Street, as it becomes Mead Lane under the arch of the bridge, which carried the double track of the Midland Railway branch line from Mangotsfield to Bath Green Park, and then on to the Somerset & Dorset line. Two girls watch, with interest and help to complete this rural picture with the last sweep of the southernmost tip of the Cotswold making its own backdrop. c1925.

Spion Kop, Jolly Sailor Lane, Saltford

Once under the railway bridge, the road bears left past a row of cottages, which have been built up from the level of the road. Beyond the road branches, with Mead Lane continuing on its way to the right as it runs parallel to the river past various properties and on to the *Jolly Sailor.* The left hand section becomes Avon Lane, a cul-de-sac that serves one or two cottages as it runs parallel with the Midland Railway Line. c1925

Unfortunately never a paying proposition, Kelston station was apparently built as a condition imposed upon the Midland Railway Company, which needed to get to Bath, and the only way was across land owned by Mr Inigo-Jones. He insisted that a station convenient to him and his family would have to be constructed, and that further more he required the right to have any train stopped for his benefit. As part of this agreement, Inigo-Jones' sisters who lived at Kelston House would exercise their right by having at least one train per year stopped, even though it meant a three-quarter mile walk through the fields to get there. c1920.

COPYRIGHT
SPION KOP. SALTFORD.

Staying on the same height as the Midland Railway and looking across the river to Gloucestershire a house known as *Spion Kop* can be seen built on a small bluff of the rolling hills, overlooking the river valley. During the Boar war there was a famous battle called Spion Kop, but exactly what the connection is between the name of the battle and the name of the house has not yet been determined. c1920

The *Jolly Sailor* Inn taken from the island created when the two locks and weir were constructed to make the river more navigable to larger crafts and allow them to travel higher up the waterway. The building was almost certainly constructed in the Georgian style when the River Avon was an important inland highway for the carrying of large and bulky items from Bristol to Bath and beyond, and with two locks to negotiate what better place than to stop and have a breather and perhaps a drink or two. c1903

19

This aerial picture shows quite clearly the *Jolly Sailor* facing the double locks and weir, together with the man made island, and surrounding buildings and boat yards including Sheppard's Yard built by the one time landlord of the aforementioned hostelry. c1925

A view looking up river, with the first set of lock gates open to the below weir level of the water, whilst the second set of gates perform their required job of maintaining the higher level. To the right of the lock, the roof and chimney of the *Jolly Sailor* can be seen as they try to rise above the surrounding trees. c1925

The Locks, Saltford

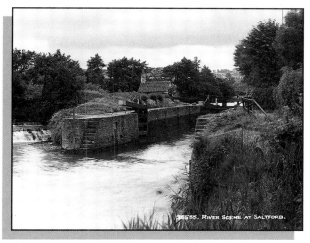

A collection of four, separate thumbnail views of the River Avon and locks adjacent to the *Jolly Sailor* watering hole. The top left-hand picture shows the nose of the down stream lock entrance alongside the weir with the gates open, to allow those who wish to venture further up river to move to the higher level. In the centre of the picture the roof of the stone built lock-keepers office can be clearly seen, c1960. Below is a close-up of the same lock, but looking down stream, and the calm of the river after it had tumbled over the drop of the weir. c1938. The top right-hand illustration shows the upper river lock gates closed to hold back the higher water, a view seen by countless mariners as they made their slow way

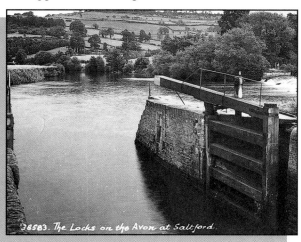

down river. Beneath, is the same pair of gates taken from the other side, with a full view of the lock-keeper's office, and the dark watermark on the stone buttresses demonstrating quite clearly the different height of the water on both sides of the weir. Note the steps leading down the side of the lock. c1938

Four more thumbnail pictures of the river at Saltford with, on the left, an aspect of its gradual curve as, in this mood, it calmly separates Somerset from Gloucestershire and swings around to the right on its way to the lower locks. High above the left-hand bank sits the *Spion Kop* house as it hangs over the properties in Mead Lane. (c1903) Because the river was tidal right up to Saltford and beyond, it was possible to ford the river by what is now known as the Shallows, hence its name. To improve the navigation of the river, weirs were constructed and locks built to hold back the upper reaches of the Avon, and its ability to be forded was lost, accordingly the river either needed to be bridged and/or a ferry service was required, or both. For many years from around 1886 to 1908, Hannah Gregory virtually single-handedly operated a foot-passenger ferry, and below she is seen around the turn of the last century, punting the empty craft across during a period of relatively slack water which, no doubt, helped her to retain her balance, the necessary slipway, and the lady's house can be seen in the background. The top right-hand picture displays the upper weir, with a collection of houseboats tied up along the Somerset bank, close to the Saltford Marina. (c1930) To the right below is the panorama of the upper weir looking from the Gloucestershire side, with more houseboats in the background, and Sheppard's Boathouse and Tea Rooms on the left. George Sheppard was, during the middle of the first decade of the twentieth century, the landlord of the *Jolly Sailor* and no doubt could see the benefits of combining the popularity of messing about in boats and the need for non-alcoholic refreshments. c1921.

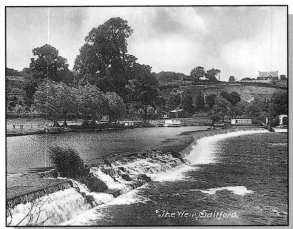

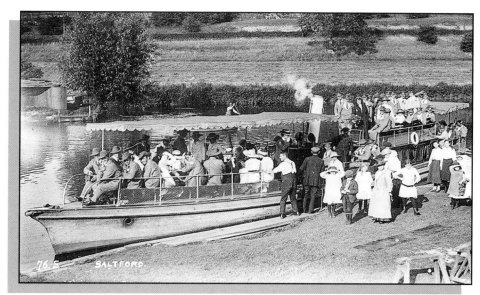

During World War 1 the nearby Newton Park Estate was used as a recuperation centre for wounded allied soldiers, under the title "Countess Temple's Hospital", and in both these two illustrations we see how the indigenous population rallied around to help these men recover from their physical and mental injuries. In the top picture a group of what appears to be Australian soldiers and a small bevy of local ladies, dressed in their summer refinery, are guests of the local steamboat company, and are about to enjoy the pleasure of a boat trip along the River Avon. Below a larger group of men who are convalescing from their wounds, have been gathered together with their nurses and female visitors for this most interesting group photograph. c1917.

Although the river around Saltford is still a very popular area of recreation, during the early part of the twentieth century when there were many less distractions and when travel to the majority meant either public transport or walking, the river was extremely fashionable, particularly to those who considered themselves to be the "out-door" type. Many of today's boat people are probably fortunate enough to own their own craft but, before, and just after the First World War, the majority of those who wish to amuse themselves on the river had little or no choice but to hire a river craft, and there were a number of businesses set up just to provide that service. In this group of pictures we can see a busy regatta underway, with men showing off their prowess as oarsmen, whilst the lady of the party maintains her unruffled Edwardian posture and the ability to keep on her quite large white hat. (c1905) Also shown is Sheppard's Boat house and Tea Rooms on one of its quiet days, c1905 and its competitor Withy's Boat Hiring Station, and Tea Room, with an anticipation of many more customers to come. (c1913)

The top illustration shows the view taken from Homefield looking down the hill through the trees and over the river valley to the lower Southwolds beyond. In the bottom left-hand corner the roof of Sheppard's Boat Yard can be seen, whilst in the centre foreground it is possible to make out the roof and the two chimneys of the eighteenth century Brass Mill. Powered by water, the mill was converted to a rolling mill to beat out the sheets of brass, and remained in operation until around 1925. The two chimneys are in respect of the annealing furnaces, which were used to help toughen the metal. c1905. Having moved further down the hill, the cameraman has been able to put a

slightly different perspective to the same view, and clearly shows the bend in the river as it meanders its way towards Bristol and the sea. Also seen in this shot are the cottages facing The Shallows. The picture in the bottom left-hand corner shows from The Shallows, the river being crossed by the Midland Railway on its original iron bridge, which was replaced in the late 1930's. In addition to carrying the railway, the bridge also had a pedestrian walkway, to provide an alternative method of crossing the river at this point. c1912.

The Shallow, Saltford

Although the river cannot be seen in this picture, it is not very far away, as it hides behind the left-hand shrubbery, and at this point runs almost parallel with the road. Many years ago this stretch of land was much lower than is shown and it was possible to ford the river at this shallow place. However, when the Great Western Railway was being constructed through Saltford during the early part of the nineteenth century, there was a considerable amount of spoil which was used to build up this low lying land to its present level. c1922.

On the right is the High Street end view of The Shallows as seen from the Midland Railway looking across the lower fields and the impressive property behind. c1925.

Saltford.

A group of smartly dressed gentlemen interrupt their afternoon stroll and pose alongside the River Avon at Saltford for a picture to be taken, at a time when everyone seemed to have more time on their hands, and life was a little more leisurely. Unfortunately, the identity of these gentlemen has so far eluded all attempts to determine who they were. c1925.

With the peaceful river flowing sedately through Saltford, the sun shining high above, and with a row of trees to provide that required amount of shade, the banks of the river along The Shallows, is an ideal place for the family to stop and enjoy a picnic as demonstrated here in this c1935 photograph.

The River Avon at Saltford.

The picture on the left is one that has been taken from the Gloucestershire side of the river looking over to the row of terraced villas, partially hidden by trees that face onto The Shallows. On the extreme left is the old Working Men's Hall, with "Rivals" standing out proudly above. c1930.

On the right the camera has been positioned on the hill running down from Homefield and, just above, in the centre foreground, the distinctive chimneys and buildings of the Brass Battery Mill. With the serpentine river showing clearly on the left, the Great Western Railway and station can be glimpsed on the right. c1910.

SALTFORD

SALTFORD

Industrial smoke mingles with domestic smoke as it hangs in the damp winter air along the valley as we look back down The Shallows from where we have come, from the zigzag lane that enables the pedestrians to reach the Great Western station which was opened as early as 1840, note the latticed footbridge on the extreme left, and the gas lamp part way up the path. c1905.

A general view looking down over Saltford Station when it was a recognized busy country station with its own goods siding, crossover points, signal box, two platforms connected by a footbridge. In this, circa 1935 picture, a number of railway wagons can be seen at the end of the single siding, (constructed in 1910) but little activity appears to be taking place. Similarly, the main road between Bath and Bristol also appears to contain very little activity, in fact the whole picture gives an air of calm peace at a time when life was much less hectic. Note the *The Ship Inn* on the right.

A closer view of the station, signal box and goods shed, with crane for work in the goods yard, which remained in operation well into the 1950's, and did not close until 1955. Note the footbridge on the right, and a glimpse of Sheppard's Tea Rooms on the left. c1912.

The original station at Saltford had relatively short platforms on both sides of the track, as can be seen in the picture on the right. Also clearly evident is the fact that when constructed during the late 1830's, Brunel still had his dream of operating a broad gauge (7ft.) system between London and Bristol, hence the wide gap between the standard gauge tracks, to which the broad gauge subsequently succumbed. In the distance the portals of the Saltford Tunnel can be clearly seen, and it was at this point between the station and the tunnel that in 1909 a major landslide occurred which brought around 100,000 tons of earth and rock down onto the track bed. At the time, an engine pulling four coaches was approaching the station through the tunnel, and before the

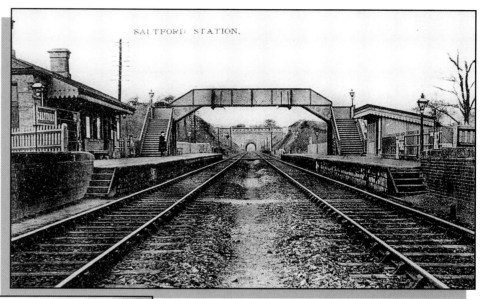

SALTFORD STATION.

RAILWAY STATION SALTFORD.

driver had time to stop, the train ploughed into the landslide and was de-railed, although fortunately nobody was seriously hurt. The line was closed for quite some while and cost a quarter of a million pounds to clear, whilst providing a great deal of short term work for scores of local men.   As the railways became more and more popular and more powerful, the trains and coaches became longer, and by the end of the nineteenth century it was realised that the existing length of Saltford station was unable to cope with the increasing number of passengers. Accordingly, both platforms were extended with the construction of wooden additions, as can be clearly seen on the left as, again the camera is pointed in the general direction of Bristol. c1925.

This is a relatively modern picture taken on the 29th September 1990, of an old building at the time when it was undergoing major restoration, having originally been *The Ship Inn*. At that time it was an important coaching inn with the left-hand cottages being part of the stable block, whilst the small building on the right was the forge. The latter was of course an essential part of the stagecoach route, and it was normal for the approaching coachman to have the horn blown to a certain pattern half a mile away to warn the farrier that his skills would be required. As travel by stagecoach was taken over by the railways, the need for an inn and stabling facilities grew less and less, and in the end the house became a farmhouse.

The land behind the above building rises quite steeply, and on this hill during the 1920's several detached and semi-detached houses were built as a speculative venture by a builder whose surname was Fox. Although well constructed, in an attractive wooded area, with a commanding view over the Avon valley, containing not only the river but also two railways and a road, with a backdrop of the rolling hills of Kelston, the properties failed to attract the expected interest in them anticipated by Mr. Fox. Possibly as a result of the depression and lack of general confidence, the house remained empty for a number of years, which resulted in them becoming known as "Fox's Folly" subsequently shortened to "The Folly" c1928.

The Glen, Saltford

A 1920's spin around "The Glen" and the "Links"

The Links, Saltford

SALTFORD WOMEN'S INSTITUTE HALL.

A summer party held in the grounds of the Saltford Women's Institute Hall, in Norman Road, with Tunnel House peering over the day's events. When this moment in time was forever frozen in a photograph, the ladies were able to indulge in showing off their refinery, the children knew how to behave, and the gentlemen were left with that rather awkward thought that they were really superfluous to the occasion, and perhaps should not have been there after all. The hut was purchased from the army as war surplus, for the cost of £68.10.0 with money loaned by the members in the form of shares, and as there was a public opening performed by the landowner, Colonel Rolleston, it is possible that this is a picture of the fete which followed immediately after ceremony. c1920.

During the early part of the twentieth century, the Bristol Tramway & Carriage Company proposed that their tram route from the city out to Brislington should be extended to run through Keynsham High Street and on to Saltford, where possibly an extension of the Bath Electric Company's system to Newton St Loe could be connected to allow trams to operate between both cities. For various reasons, this proposal never got off the ground and instead by 1906, it was decided to substitute the trams with omnibuses, with the terminus identified at *The Crown Inn* Saltford. Here we see a solid tyred double deck bus outside the inn on what is possibly the inaugural journey, with a large notice in the bus window advertising the new route, and the crew immaculately dressed, watched by a number of interested spectators.

Probably also taken during 1906, the new route has settled down to become an every day event, and little interest is being taken of this bus (AE770) as it waits for passengers and the time to start its journey back to Brislington. Note the two horse-drawn carriages and a number of bicycles waiting outside for their owners to finish their refreshments, and the vehicle on the extreme right, which could be an early locally produced car, based upon a horse-drawn carriage frame.

Having moved away from Saltford in the direction of Bath there is, a mile or so along the road, another important nineteenth century hostelry *"The Globe Inn"* still open to the many travellers as today they rush by having negotiated a large roundabout on their way to the nearby large cities and the smaller villages. Originally the main road swept up from Newton Meadows on up the gentle hill to Marksbury and beyond, whilst at right angles the road from Warminster crossed, as it continued to Bristol. Having been built at a strategic cross road, the inn became a focal point of travel as can be seen in this picture where a group of around twenty-seven well dressed men, all sporting flowers in their button holes have stopped for light refreshments, provided by the landlord, T.W.Jose. Their horse-drawn carriage contains wooden seats, and is framed with curtains and, no doubt, an overthrow just in case the summer weather should produce the odd shower or two.. c1910.

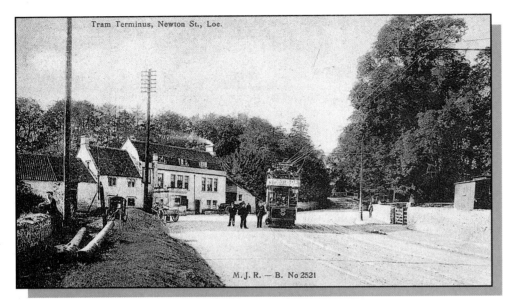

Tram Terminus, Newton St., Loe.

M. J. R. — B. No 2521

Although well out in the countryside, the importance of *The Globe Inn* as a focal transport point did not go un-noticed by the Bath Electric Traction Company, who decided that they would extend their tram route from the main line Great Western railway station in Bath out to the inn at Newton St Loe. Promoted in 1899 by the Bath & District Light Railway, the route was constructed and opened by 1904. Shown here are two photographs of the countryside terminus in the early days of its use with, on the left, a somewhat pristine and posed picture of Bath tram No.30 fully loaded with passengers, and a crew eager to show off their smart uniforms in the summer sunshine, on what might be the first return trip of the new service. At one time it had been proposed that instead of terminating at this spot, the tracks should continue beyond the tram and to the right, and on through to probably *The Crown Inn* at Saltford where it was to join the extended Bristol Tramway Company's rails from Brislington but, unfortunately, the whole scheme was abandoned. On the right the second picture has been taken many months after the route was opened, and no longer is there any euphoria of trams running out into the countryside. No.33 routinely stands amongst the autumn debris, and with a few passengers, waits with both crew at the front for its picture to be taken, before it trundles off along the long Newton Meadows, over Newbridge Bridge and on in to the city. Note the substantial, and rather ugly "carbuncle" porch which once defaced the front of *"The Globe Inn"*. c1904

Following the collapse of the plans to extend both tramways for an intended meeting at *The Crown Inn,* the Bristol Tramway & Carriage Company decided to expand its recently created Brislington to Saltford bus service, onto *The Globe Inn* at Newton St Loe, thus facilitating those passengers who wished to travel between both cities, even if it did necessitate changing from bus to tram, at least there was an inn where travellers could await their connection. On the right is a picture of one of BTC's Thornycroft type omnibuses, with a United electric Co double deck body (AE236), posing outside of *The Globe* in the late summer sunshine with its immaculately dressed crew, and possibly two officials from the company, in September 1906.

One of the problems with open top double deck buses, certainly in those early days of leaf springs, more reminiscent of a horse-drawn wagon than a motorized vehicle, to which was added the inflexibility of solid tyres, meant that the whole body swayed with the unpredictable movement of the bus, particularly as it negotiated the bends in the road. This movement was greatly exaggerated to those passengers seating on the top deck, and with the added need of having to avoid over-hanging trees as they were swept along the countryside, double deck buses were not popular on this route. Accordingly the bus company decided that they would convert some of their vehicles to single deck versions, and in the lower picture is an example of one of those conversions, also seen at *The Globe* terminus in another posed picture. September 1907.

POST OFFICE & SCHOOL.
NEWTON ST. LOE.

Moving up the hill from *The Globe* and turning right we come to the almost hidden, but very attractive village of Newton St Loe, all part of the Duchy of Cornwall's estate. On the left is the short road that leads to the parish church of Holy Trinity with, in the top picture, the old Post Office with a postman's bicycle parked outside, whilst opposite is the old village pump. At the time that this picture was taken, around 1904, the sub-postmaster was John Mercer. In the lower view, the camera has been moved across the road and is looking more directly at the Post Office, which by now has the added advantage of having a wall mounted letter box. The old pump has been removed, although the surrounding railings remain, but with so little traffic they would not have been considered to create any form of hazard. Behind the two large elm trees is the property known as Stonewalls with, beyond, Holy Trinity church. c1910

Post Office & Church
Newton St Loe.

School House Newton St Loe.

Having arranged for the seventeen or so children and teacher to step outside, the cameraman had grouped them across the road in the summer shade and captured a moment in the social history of this small village as, no doubt, when this picture was taken (c1910) all of the local children of junior school age were represented. How much the world was to change, as they grew older. Their school building stands behind, and above the doorway in the porch is an inscription that reads:

"This free school was built and endowed ate the charge of Richard Jones of Stawey in the County of Somerset, anno domini 1698."

Parish Church, Newton Saint Loe.

It is possible the coach nearest the church belongs to the Langton family, and is waiting to take one or more of them back to their ancestral home after the evening service. Both drivers look as though they have been there for some little while and are perhaps wondering when they are likely to be able to sit down to their own evening meal. c1907

41

A young lady in her summer best stands outside the entrance of Holy Trinity Church, which is built of stone in the Early Decorated Style, and consists (as illustrated below) of a chancel, a nave of five bays, aisles, north and south porch, and an embattled tower with pinnacles. Internally there are some handsome tablets to the Langton family. Both pictures were taken c1905. The young lady in the picture is something of a mystery, as she appears in a number of photographs

of Newton St Loe, some of which have subsequently been produced with her image having been removed. This is illustrated quite clearly in a photograph printed later in this book, and will be dealt with again on that particular page. She obviously knew the photographer, and was friendly with him at the time that the photographs were taken, but did she do something to upset him at a later stage? Is this a mystery that has an answer?

With his back to the church, the photographer has swung around his camera and we are now looking back the way we have come, with the school on the right. The impressive building in the centre background is the Duchy of Cornwall office. c1905.

Having moved away from the church, there is next to the Duchy of Cornwall office, a turning on the right as seen below, the Rectory is reached from this lane. Both pictures were probably taken around 1904.

RECTORY, NEWTON ST. LOE.

NEWTON ST. LOE.

PARK ENTRANCE & LODGE, NEWTON ST. LOE.

NEWTON ST. LOE.

Continuing down the previously pictured lane where it forms a 'T' junction, there is the 'back' entrance to Newton Park House with, despite its apparent relegated position, a fine Lodge House to guard against any unwelcome guests and/or tradesmen who might wish to gain access to the ancestral home of the Langton family. For those visitors who were not acceptable, a turn to the left would bring them to this pair of delightful thatched roof cottages, on their journey back to the village. c1906.

The Fountain, Newton St Loe.

At the heart of this sleepy village is a small oblong shape that contained, at the time that the picture was taken, two mature trees, and a fountain as seen in the above moment in time when the summer sunshine enabled the broad branches to cast their cooling shade, and add to the peacefulness of rural Newton. On the right is the shop belonging to "Ann Simpkins ~ Baker & Grocer, licensed to sale Beer and Stout to be consumed off the premises". c1920.

THE FOUNTAIN, NEWTON ST. LOE.

This illustration shows the reverse of that shown on page 46, with Ann Simpkins' shop now on the left. In the picture there is the same young lady as can be seen standing outside of the church, and quite obviously she was walking around the village at the same time as, or possibly even with the photographer. However when copies of the above picture were subsequently printed, the lady has disappeared, (see back cover) but a closer inspection shows that she has in fact been shaded out, although not very well, as the photographer has left her shoes just visible in the reprints. c1905

With the photographer having acted as the local pied piper, he has managed to gather together as many of the village children as possible, perhaps with the inducement of a sweet or two in days when such action would not have been frowned upon, and carefully arranged them with impunity across the road junction, to stand at attention (although a couple of the children presumably did not quite understand what he meant), on a cold winter's day. With the trees bare of leaves, the thatched roof cottages can be easily seen. c1904.

VILLAGE, NEWTON ST. LOE.

Newton Saint Loe.

M. J. R. — B. No 2519

Summer has returned, and the trees are in full foliage, as a pony and trap are positioned as though they have just come up the lane although, of course, the photographer, with the limitation of his equipment, wished to avoid as much movement as possible. c1904

This is a rare picture of the Newton St Loe Forge, which was positioned ideally under the spreading chestnut tree, almost at the top of the hill opposite The Mount, and the farrier, having no doubt been asked to stand outside of his workshop with one of his charges to have their picture taken by the photographer who, you will remember, was walking around the village with a young lady in a white blouse, dark skirt, and a light coloured wide brimmed hat, as clearly seen in two previous pictures. However it will be recalled that re-prints of the reversed fountain illustration have been touched-up so that the lady is shaded out. A closer look at the wall in the background shows quite clearly that when the photograph was taken the young lady was walking by, but by the time that this and the other prints were produced she needed to be eliminated, one wonders why? What had she done that so upset the photographer? c1905

"The Mount" c1927

"The Hayes" c1935.

HAYES, NEWTON ST. LOE.

PARK ENTERANCE & LODGE, NEWTON ST. LOE.

With a larger lodge house, and a much more elaborate set of gates and supporting pillars, this tells all who arrive that this is the front and main entrance to the Newton Park Estate, the home of the Langton family. c1923

Newton St Loe, from the Park Drive

NEWTON PARK HOUSE BATH.

Take a pictorial trip around Newton Park Estate. c1930

The Tower, Park House, Newton St Loe.

Newton Park, Flower Gardens.

Looking along the main road towards Marksbury, on a particularly quite, peaceful traffic free, summers day around 1924, when it was pleasant to stroll along in the sunshine, and it was perfectly safe to invite children to stand and idle in the middle of the road, certainly something not to be recommended today.

Corston Village, Nr. Bath.

M.J.R. — B. N

Having walked on up the hill along the rather muddy road and passed the rank of properties on the left, the photographer has turned the camera around ninety degrees and is now looking back the way we have come. Once again he has invited some of the locals to animate the picture and stand outside their property or, the more favourite position, in the middle of the road with, on this occasion, the family pets. Note the Ale and Porter store partially hidden behind the heavy foliage. c1922.

Corston Village, Nr. Bath.

By the state of the road, this picture was almost certainly taken on the same day as the one shown on page 54, with the photographer having walked a hundred yards or so further up the hill, and again having turned the camera around ninety degrees has captured the village school on the left, the last row of cottages in Corston in the centre background, and a lone man pushing his wheelbarrow, where else but in that time honoured place, the middle of the road. Whatever caused this custom to fall out of use? c1922

Shown above is the exterior and interior of All Saints Church Corston, taken around 1914. On the back of the left-hand card there are congratulations Claude C Parker, Rector of Corston for arranging for the first peel (after the First World War) to be made on the bells of All Saints, 30 December 1918. To the right is the village Post Office c1920.

The main road from Marksbury to Bath as it passes through Corston, and the site of "The Hanging Tree" c1910.

Corston, The Hanging Tree (Som)

THE HANGING TREE, CORSTON.

Although the reverse view of the above, this is a more up-to-date view of the same place, as the road sweeps away to the right and on towards Bath. c1935.

The centre of Corston village with six children of varying ages asked by the photographer to stand, somewhat, as it has turned out, self-consciously across the road and by the side streets, in a posture so reminiscent of that time and age. Although this card was postally used as a 1909 New Year's greeting, the picture almost certainly dates back to around 1905.

CORSTON   MANOR FARM

Manor Farm is the house where the poet Southey once lived, whilst he went to school in the village, although it is reputed that he did not enjoy the experience. Note the steps on the right of the gate in the lower picture, designed to help the rider get on and off their horse. c1928

House at Corston, Bath. (Where Southey lived).

Along the road between Corston and Marksbury stands this somewhat isolated shop with off sale facilities, which eagerly advertises its principal's prime product. Other refreshments could also be obtained here for the passing traveller. c1930. Although this book ends at this place, a further one is planned to take the reader back in time to Marksbury and beyond.